Columba -
The Celtic Dove

The prophetic
and supernatural
ministry of
Columba of Iona
A.D. 521-A.D. 597

Kathie Walters

1st Printing February 1999

Published by
GOOD NEWS MINISTRIES
220 Sleepy Creek Road
Macon, Georgia 31210

Layout and Graphics by
Quality Computer Works
◇<

saylor@hom.net

OTHER TITLES
By Kathie Walters:

Living in the Supernatural
The Spirit of False Judgment
The Visitation
Parenting-By the Spirit
Celtic Flames

GOOD NEWS MINISTRIES
220 Sleepy Creek Road
Macon, Georgia 31210
Phone (912) 757-8071
Fax   (912) 757-0136

e-mail: goodnews@hom.net
www.goodnews.netministries.org

Dedicted to

Gwen Shaw,
Founder - End-Time Handmaidens

Iverna Tompkins,
Teacher, Instructor

GODS'S GENERALS - AND MY HEROES

Forward

Like many people who experienced spiritual renewal during the charismatic movement of the 1970's, I always assumed that the church had been in some sort of deep freeze until the outpouring of the Spirit that occurred at the beginning of this century. In fact, most Charismatics and Pentecostals today believe that it was not until 1901 - during the revival in Topeka, Kansas - that modern-day signs, wonders and miracles were restored to the church. You will learn in this book, however, that God did not withdraw His power from His people at any point in history.

In every generation, the Holy Spirit has been working among God's people. And in every era, the signs, wonders and miracles of the book of Acts have pointed humanity to the Savior. In pre-Christian Ireland, at a time when the darkness of druid idolatry held a nation in spiritual bondage, God empowered His messenger, Columba, with the gifts of the Holy Spirit. A spiritual fire was kindled by the ministry of this prophet of God, and the warmth of it can still be felt today—many centuries later. I pray that this account of Columba's life will spark a renewed desire in you to make the same kind of impact for God in your generation.

- J. Lee Grady
Executive Director, Charisma Magazine

Many thanks to
Patty and Bunty
for your practical help
and encouragement.

Many thanks also to Maureen Eha.

CONTENTS

CONTENTS (cont.)

CONTENTS (cont.)

PREFACE

When I was visiting Great Britain in June of 1998 I felt that I had some divine appointments. One of them was with a book-which I came across by "accident" in Ireland.

The result of that appointment is this manuscript. It contains some accounts from the life of Saint Columba. These testimonies were recorded by Saint Adamnan (A.D. 679-A.D. 704) as told to him by eyewitnesses and translated from the Latin by Bishop MacCarthy of Kerry, Professor J. T. Fowler and the Bishop of Brechin. Wentworth Hughes with the assistance of Rev. George Cormack, of St. Ethelreda's, Ely House, Holborn did a translation in the early 1900's.

As I read through the pages I was gripped by Columba's holiness and the operation of faith in his life. Adamnan's accounts of incredible prophesies, wondrous miracles and healings, and angelic encounters, made me want so much to put this into the hands of present-day God-seekers, to encourage them to press on into God. If God's people lived in this kind of anointing in the early centuries, should we not have it today? Even more so, as the church has had so much more revelation of truth down through the ages.

Kathie Walters

ABOUT COLUMBA-

First Christian missionary to the pagan tribes of North Britain and founder of the monastery of Iona

Columba was born at Gartan (Little Field) on the night in which Buite, the Founder of Monasterboise, died, 7th December A.D. 521. His father was Fedhlimidh (Phelim), a chieftain of the clan of O'Donnell. His great-grandfather was Nial Naighiallach, King of Ireland from A.D. 379-A.D. 405. Columba's mother was Ethne, eleventh in descent from Cathair Mor, King of Leinster, so on both sides of the family, he was from royal lineage. He was eligible for the kingship of Eriu, and according to the family heritage, it was offered him. But he abandoned it for God.

Garten, his birthplace, is on a hillside, at the foot of which are three lakes. Cruithnechan, the priest, baptized him at Tulach Dubbglaise (Temple Douglas) by the two names of Dolum (dove) and Crimthain (wolf). At the time of Columba's birth Justinian was Emperor of Constantinople, and Benedict had founded his monastic order at Monte Cassino.

The Roman legions had been withdrawn from Britain for 100 years and the Angles, Jutes and Saxons were pouring into Britain in waves of invasions, driving the Christianized Britains westward. In Ireland, Christianity had been established in many areas.

An Irish child of royal birth was always brought up by foster parents, and Columba's foster parent was the minister Cruithnechan, and he was also brought up by the O'Firghils. His childhood, was spent with them at Doire Ethne. While he was under the care of Cruithnechan his mind became deeply conscious of spiritual things, which was to lead to great results, and he was given the name of Colum-Kill (Colum of the kill, or cell) because he so often came out from the cell in which he used to read the Psalms, according to the ancient Irish record in Leabhar Breac.

Columba, after leaving Cruithnechan, became a pupil at Moville, County Down, the Ecclesiastical School founded by Finnian in A.D. 540. There he was ordained a deacon. After leaving Moville he went to Master Gemman, an aged Bard of Leinster, and there he confirmed his love for the old poetic tales of Ireland. It was while he was with Gemman that he and Gemman tried to prevent the murder of a young girl.

Columba went to the monastic school of the Abbot Finnian, the wise tutor of Erin's saints, the most famous in Ireland, founded in A.D. 520. Twelve of Finnian's disciples, including Columba, were known as the twelve apostles of Erin. On the day of his arrival, Columba asked the Abbot Finnian where he should put up his hut. "At the door of the church," was the answer. Columba built his cell some distance away from the door. "You have not obeyed my directions," said the Abbott. "It is true that I have not done so," replied Columba, "But the door will at a future time be here."

As the monastery grew in extent and importance, the door of the church was where Columba had predicted. He was ordained a priest at Colard by Bishop Etchen. After his ordination he went with three friends to Glasnevinm, near Dublin, where Mobbi, one of his fellow students, had a school. The pupils were later dispersed because of an outbreak of Yellow Plague. Columba returned to his native province of Ulster, praying as he crossed the Bio (Moyola water), that the plague might be stayed.

A.D. 545: Columba founded the monastery of Derry. A fortified hill was given him by an admiring kinsman and there he built his first church. Afterwards the hill was known for a thousand years as Daire Columkille: it then took a prefix from the home of its conquerors and was called Londonderry. Now it is known by its oldest universal name Daire (Derry). A lane called Longtower still marks the locality of the church built by Columba.

A.D. 545-A.D. 562: Columba founded many churches and monasteries. One of them was the monastery of Kells in Meath, and from it is named another famous book, "The Book of Kells," which is beautiful in its ornamentation and elaboration.

The most remote of Columba's monasteries was that of Glen Columkille, in the western most part of Ulster. Here, on the north side of the glen, are the ruins of Columba's church and traces of the monastic building.

Large donations of land, skillfully tilled by monks, enabled the monasteries of Erin to grant free education, food, clothing and books to thousands who flocked to their halls. The monastic schools for three centuries were regarded as the chief centers for education. In the fifth and sixth centuries, amidst the dreadful shock of the fall of the Roman Empire and the desolation of Europe by barbarous hordes, Ireland became the asylum of learning, and monks from Ireland then carried the torch to the devastated regions of Gaul and Germany.

A.D. 561-A.D. 563: THE 'EXILE' OF COLUMBA. Columba's greatest work was to be done elsewhere though, among people who, while unaffected by the fall of the Roman Empire and by invasion, were sunk in paganism -- the Picts of Alban who dwelt beyond the Grampions, in the eastern parts of what is now Scotland. It was in A.D. 563 that Columba left Ireland, two years after a great battle between Diarmait, King of Ireland, and Columba's kinsmen (the Clan Neill), which was fought at Culdreimhne, six miles north of Sligo in A.D. 561. It is said that Columba himself mustered the Clan Neill for war against King Diarmait for the purpose of avenging two grievances against him. One grievance was that Diarmait had slain Columba's clansman, the young Prince Curnan. The other was a judgment that Columba considered unjust, given against him by Diarmait, in the matter of ownership of a book. The incident is related by the Rev. John Golden: "In Columba's thirty-ninth year, while visiting at Clonard, he secretly made a copy of a beautiful book of the Psalms, kept by the Abbot Finian in the church. The Abbot soon discovered it and demanded the copy as his right. The book had cost Columba many a sleepless night, and he refused to surrender it. The disputants appealed to King Diarmait. 'To every cow belongs her calf,' was his judgment. Very grieved over the loss of his copy, Columba boldly exclaimed, 'This is an unjust decision, O Diarmait, and I will be avenged!'" This manuscript is now in the Library of the Royal Irish Academy.

THE BATTLE. It is said that King Diarmait imprisoned Columba at Tara, but he escaped and made for his home in Tyrconnell. His kindred took up arms for his cause and the battle was fought at Cooldrummon, near Sligo. King Diarmait was defeated, and there was a great slaughter. Diarmait then called a synod at Teltown in Meath, which excommunicated Columba. After preaching and baptizing in Erin, he went on a pilgrimage with twelve disciples to Iona. At a later date King Brude sanctioned Columba's right to title of the little island.

COLUMBA'S MONASTIC SYSTEM required strict submission to a rule that enforced observance of religious duty, ascetic practice and self-denial. The practice of making the sign of the cross is constantly mentioned by Adamnan as a very important part of the monastic system of Iona. They fasted on Wednesdays and Fridays. Those who adopted this monastic life under Columba were called "Soldiers of Christ," and their principal was to obedience, celibacy, (very strictly enjoined and enforced by Columba), caution and reason in speech, humility, and especially developed in Iona- hospitality and kindness to animals.

COLUMBA'S FREQUENT JOURNEYS. It is important to remember that the monks would have frequently visited the other islands to preach to the heathen. Columba realized that if the Pictish tribes were to be converted to Christ, he must begin with their king. So Columba set out in A.D. 565 on the longest journey he had made since reaching Iona. His companions were Comgall and Canice, Irish Picts who would have felt more at home with the king than Columba.

Adamnan tells how the king barred his gate against the mission and how the druids opposed him in every possible way, but how the cross triumphed in that citadel of paganism. Those whom the Caesars could not subdue were brought under the yoke of Christ. Here among the heathen and druidic powers, Columba preached everywhere, planted churches, and established schools. His preaching was confirmed by many miracles. The Orkney Islands, the Hebrides and the Faroes heard and accepted the gospel. On distant Iceland, missions were established, and even within the lifetime of Columba, Iona was able to send forth missionaries to Northumbria, the Isle of Man and South Britain.

A.D. 574: AEDHAN IS ORDAINED KING OF BRITISH DALRIADA BY COLUMBA. Columba's connections to the royal family of Ireland and his kinship with many of the noblest families in Ireland, made him an important factor in the history of northern Britain. An event then occurred that shows the height of power Columba attained. Conall, son of Comgall, king of the British Dalriada, died that and according to the law, he should have been succeeded by his cousin Eogan, whose claim was favored by Columba. In an angelic encounter however Columba was directed to ordain another cousin, Aedhan.

A.D. 575: THE CONVENTION OF DRUMCEATT. In the year A.D. 575 Aedh, son of Ainmire, king of Ireland, summoned a great convention. All the lesser kings and heads of tribes, the principal clergy of Ireland, Columba and the newly consecrated King of Dalriada, Aiden were present. There were three reasons that Columba and his company attended. (1) For the releasing of Scannlan Mor, son of Cennfaeladh, King of Ossary, in Leinster who was hostage in the hands of Aedh, Columba being surety for him; (2) For the staying of the bards (poets) in Ireland, for they were near to being banished on account of their burdensomeness; (3) For pacification between the men of Ireland and Alban, about Dalriada. In all of these objectives, Columba was successful.

SCANNLAN THE THIRSTY. The account of the release of Scannlan is one of the most curious passages in the *Old Irish Life of Columba.* The end of the year found Scannlan still a prisoner in the hands of Aedh. He was not released, and no hostage was accepted in his stead. A wicker hut was constructed round him with no passage out, save a way through which a little salted food and a small allowance of ale was given him. Fifty warriors guarded him, and there were nine chains upon him in the hut. When he would see anyone going past, he would cry out for a drink.

These things were reported to Columba in Iona, and he wept greatly at what he heard and was prompted by it to go to the convention and demand the release of Scannlan. "I shall not release him, until he dies in the hut where he is," said King Aedh. Columba replied, "We will not pursue this subject further, but if it be pleasing to God, may it be he that takes off my shoes tonight at Matins in whatsoever place I be." Then Columba left and went to the Dubb-regles, the Black Abbey church at Derry. Not long after he left, a thunderbolt fell among the members of the assembly at Drumceatt, and they all fell to the ground. Scannlan, set free by an angel, made his way straight to Black Rock Church at Derry, and Scannlan assisted in taking off Columba's shoes at worship." He was later made King of Ossory and granted to Columba a tribute from the Ossorians every seventh year.

THE "FULL HABITATION" OF COLUMBA. Not one stone is left upon another of Columba's church in Derry, "My Derry," as he called it;

> "My Derry, my little oak grove,
> My dwelling, and my little cell."

What Adamnan says of Columba is still true, "Though he lived in this small and remote island of the British Isles, not only has his name become known throughout the whole of Ireland and Britain, but has also reached even to Gaul and to Italy and triangular Spain, and also to the city of Rome. And much further has this honorable ministry extended, passing over vast oceans and to islands and continents, of which the good Abbot never dreamed.

But it is to Iona, that standpoint from which, he declared to the heathen the gospel of the Lord, that we turn with the greatest affection and reverence. Iona, where Columba set up his everlasting rest, from which he sent back to Ireland a messenger bearing his benediction:

'Carry with thee, thou noble youth,
My blessing and my benediction,
One-half upon Erin, sevenfold, and half on Alba
Take my blessing with thee to the west;
Broken is my heart in my breast,
Should sudden death overtake me
It is from my great love of the Gaedhil;
Gaedhil! Gaedhil! Beloved name.'

"And there was not born of Gaedhil," says the old biographer,

"A man more illustrious, or wise, or of better family than Columkille; there came not of them any person who was more modest and humble or more lowly. One of the greatest of those revered by the Gael and Briton is Columkille, the Dove of the church."

ABOUT ADAMNAN.
(First writer of the Columba story)

Born in A.D. 624 in Drumhome, Donegal, Ireland, Adamnan became a monk at the monastery there and later in Iona, of which he became the ninth Abbot in A.D. 679. He gave sanctuary to Aldrid when the crown of Northumbria was in dispute after the death of Aldrid's father, King Oswy. In A.D. 686. When Aldrid ascended the throne, Adamnan visited him to secure the release of Irish prisoners.

Two years later Adamnan visited several English monasteries and was induced by Ceofrid to adopt the Roman calendar for Easter. This had previously been fought by Columba. He succeeded in getting women exempt from war at the Council of Birr, and women and children not be taken prisoner or killed. It was called "Adamnan's Law."

Adamnan was in Ireland in A.D. 692 and again in A.D. 697. It is believed that Adamnan wrote the *Life of Columba* in between these two visits. He seems to have remained in Ireland until A.D. 704, when he returned to his monastery in Iona and soon afterwards died. The Rev. George

McCormack, who assisted Wentworth Huyshe in preparing the 1905 English version of *Life of Columba,* believed that Adamnan wrote in Latin but thought in Irish; hence the inflection of proper names according to the Irish grammar.

PART ONE - PROPHETIC GIFT

PROPHECY CONCERNING ERNENE, SON OF CRASEN.

Columba stayed for some months in the midland part of Ireland, founding the monastery which is called in Irish Dair-Mag. He visited the brethren who were dwelling in the Clonoension monastery of St. Ceran. When they heard of his arrival, all of them from around the fields, together with those within the monastery, followed Abbot Alither and went out to meet Columba. He was greeted warmly and with reverence, and singing praises, they conducted him to the church.

They bound together a canopy of poles, carried by four men, and walked around Columba as he went. This was done to keep the crowd from jostling him. At the same time, a servant lad, of very low birth and not pleasing to his elders, hid himself as much as he could and came behind, that he might secretly touch the border of Columba's cloak. But it was not hidden from Columba, for what his bodily eyes could not see, he perceived by the Spirit. He stopped suddenly, and stretching out his hand behind him, he took hold of the boy's neck and drew him around and set him in front of him. And while those around said, "Send him away," Columba prophesied, saying, "Let him be, brethren, let him be." But to the frightened boy he said, "Son, open your mouth and put out your tongue." And Columba stretched out his hand, blessed it and said, "Although this boy now seems to you worthless, yet let no one despise him for that. For from this time he will greatly please you; and he will increase from day to day in virtue and wisdom, and great will be his progress in your community. His tongue shall be gifted by God with wholesome doctrines and eloquence."

Adamnan says that this boy was Ernene, son of Crasen, who later became famous and respected among all the churches of Ireland. And it was he who reported these words prophesied by St. Columba, to the Abbot Seghine, my predecessor.

THE BATTLE OF THE MIATHI.

At another time, when Columba was in the island of Iona, he suddenly said to his servant Doirmit, "Ring the bell." The brethren, roused by the sound, ran quickly to the church, Columba himself going before. And there on bended knees, he said to them, "Now let us pray the Lord earnestly for the people and for King Aidan, for in this hour they are entering battle." And after an interval, Columba went out of the oratory, and looking up to the heavens he said, "Now are the barbarians scattered, and although it is an unhappy one, yet to Aiden is given the victory." Columba also prophesied as to the number of slain of Aiden's army as being 303 men.

Notes:
"Ring the bell . " It was a handbell. Warren (Celtic liturgy) says that a bell of St. Columba, possibly this same bell is still in existence in the collection of the late Mr. John Bell of Dungannon.

THE SONS OF KING AIDAN.

At another time, before a battle, Columba questioned King Aidan as to his successor in the kingdom. He replied that he did not know which of his three sons should reign, Arthur, or Eochoid Find or Domingart. Columba prophesied, "None of these three will be the ruler, for they will fall in battle, but now if you have any other younger sons, let them come to me, and him whom God will choose for king will suddenly rush to my bosom."

And when they were called in, Eochoid Buide ran to him according to the word, and lay in his lap. And immediately Columba kissed and blessed him, and said to King Aidan, "This is your survivor, and he is to reign after you, and his sons will reign after him."

And in due season all things were completely fulfilled. For Arthur and Eochoid Find were slain in the battle of Miathi. Domingart was killed in battle in Saxonia. Eochoid Buide succeeded to the throne after his father.

DOMHNALL, SON OF AEDH.

Domhnall, the son of Aedh, while yet a boy was brought by his foster parents to Columba on Drum Ceatt, and looking at him, Columba asked, "Whose son is this?" And they answered, "This is Domhnall, son of Aedh, who has been brought to you that he may receive your blessing." When Columba had blessed him, he said, "This one will survive after all his brethren, and be a very famous king; nor will he ever be delivered into his enemie's hands, but will die peacefully in old age and in his own house, in the presence of his close friends." And all these things were truly fulfilled, according to the prophecy.

Notes:

"Domhnall, Son of King Aedh." - Died in A.D. 598

"Drumceatt or Dromocheta" - the Ridge of Ceatt of Keth (a mans' name), in Derry. The famous convention of Drumceatt, mentioned later by Adamnan, was held there in A.D. 575.

"Foster-parent "- Clerical guardian

"Die in his own house" - It was very unusual for an Irish Chieftain to die peacefully, making the prophecy more remarkable.

THE SON OF KING DIARMAIT.

When Columba was staying for some days in Ireland, he spoke prophetically to Aedh, who came to him, "You should be careful, my son, lest by doing a murderous sin, you lose the prerogative, predestined by God for you, of the monarchy of the kingdom of all Ireland. If ever you do commit this sin, you will not enjoy the whole kingdom, but only a part of it, and only for a short time." And these words of Columba were fulfilled, for after Aedh treacherously killed Suibone, son of Colman, he held that part of the kingdom for only four years and three months.

TWO BOYS.

Another time two men came to Columba on the Isle of Iona. One of them, Meldan by name, asked Columba about his son, who was present, concerning his future. Columba spoke; "Is not today the Sabbath (Saturday)? Your son will die next Friday, and a week from today he will be buried here."

Then the other peasant, Glasderc by name, also inquired as to the son who was with him and heard these words from Columba, "Your son, Ernane, will see his grandchildren and be buried an old man in this island." All of these things regarding both boys were in their times fulfilled.

COLCA, SON OF AEDH DRAIGNICHE, CONCERNING A SECRET SIN OF HIS MOTHER.

At one time, Columba questioned Colca, staying with him in the island of Iona, about his mother, asking whether she was religious. Colca replied, "I have always known my mother to be well conducted and of good report." Columba then spoke prophetically, "Set out quickly, God willing, for Ireland. Question your mother very earnestly regarding a certain very great secret sin of hers, which she will confess to no man." And Colca, hearing this, obeyed, and went over to Ireland. His mother, when closely questioned by him, denied at length any sin, but finally confessed, and repenting, she was healed. She wondered greatly at what had been revealed to Columba concerning her.

But Colca returned to Columba and stayed with him some

days. He afterwards inquired about his own end and heard this answer, "In your own country which you love, you will be prior of some church for many years, and at some time you will see your cellarer making merry at a supper with his friends. And when you see him whirling the jug by the neck, know that in a short time you will die." This prophecy was fulfilled in all respects.

Notes:

"Colca " - Colgan - Colcu.." - an Irish saint.

"The prior of some church" - The Latin is "Primarius." The parish church of Kilcolgan, in Galway, derives its name from Colgan.

THE GREAT WHALE.

On a certain day a brother, Berach by name, proposing to sail to the Ethican island (Tiree), came to Columba in the morning and asked for a blessing. Columba looked at him and said, "Son, take very great care today; don't attempt to cross over the broad ocean in a direct course for the Ethican land, but rather, go around, and sail by the smaller islands. The reason is that, terrified by some great whale, you may narrowly escape." And Berach, having received the blessing, departed and, going into the ship, set off, not heeding the word. Crossing the wider reaches of the Ethican sea, he and the sailors who were there looked and saw a whale of immense size, lifting itself up like a mountain on the surface. Then the rowers, greatly terrified, turned back and hardly escaped from the commotion of waves arising from the movement of the whale. Remembering Columba's word, they marveled.

On that same day also, another brother Baithene, was about to sail. Columba told him in the morning about the whale, saying, "Last night at midnight a great whale raised itself from the depth of the sea, and it will lift itself on the surface of the ocean today between Iona and the Ethican islands." And Baithene answered him and said, "I and that beast are under the power of God." "Go in peace," said Columba, "Your faith in Christ shall defend you from this danger."

Then Baithene, having received Columba's blessing, sailed out from the harbor, and his companions saw the whale and were greatly alarmed. Baithene, undaunted, and with both hands uplifted, blessed the waters and the whale. And in the same moment the whale plunged beneath the surface and disappeared and did not rise again.

A CERTAIN MAN'S SINS.

At another time Columba aroused the brethren in the dead of night, and when they were gathered together in the church, he said, "Let us pray to the Lord, for in this hour some terrible sin has been committed, for which the judgment of the Lord is very much to be feared." And of this sin he spoke the next day to a few who were questioning him about it, saying, "After a few months that unhappy fellow will come to the isle of Iona with Lugaid, who knows nothing about it."

After some months, Columba spoke to Diormit, saying, "Rise quickly; Lugaid is drawing near. Tell him to cast out the wretched man who is with him in the ship, lest he treads on our island." And obeying the command, Diomitt went to the sea and told Lugaid, as his ship was drawing close to the island, the words of Columba concerning the man. When he heard this, the man swore that he would never take food with others unless he first saw Columba and spoke with him.

Returning to Columba, Diormit related to him the words the man had spoken. Columba went down to the haven where Bethany was suggesting that they receive the repentance of the man, quoting passages of Scripture in evidence. Columba said, "Bethany, this man has committed fratricide after the manner of Cain." Then the man on his bended knee promised that he would fulfill the acts of repentance according to the rules of the monastery. And Columba said to him, "If for twelve years you serve among the Britains, and do not return to Ireland, God will prove your repentance for your sin."* Columba then turned to his own people and said, "This man is a son of perdition, who will not fulfill his promise, but will soon return to Scotia (Ireland) and in a short time be slain by his enemies."

All things came to pass according to the prophecy, for the man, returning to Ireland, fell into the hands of his enemies and was slain in the region of Lea. He was of the descendants of Turte.

Notes:

"Lugaid" - The messenger of the monastery.

"Lea (Li)" - near Colraine.

* The Celtic church believed strongly that if there was real repentance, there must be proof in the acts of the repentant.

THE INK HORN.

On another day, a shout was raised from the other side of the strait of the isle of Iona, and Columba, sitting in his little hut, heard the shout, and said, "The man who is shouting beyond the strait is not refined, for today he will spill and upset my ink horn." And Diormit, his attendant, hearing this word, stood for a while in the front gate awaiting the arrival of the troublesome guest, that he might guard the ink horn.

But for some cause Diormit left, and after he had gone the guest arrived. And in his eagerness to greet Columba, he upset the ink horn, which was overturned by his sleeve.

PROPHECY REGARDING A CITY IN THE ROMAN EMPIRE.

At another time, Lugbe, of the clan Mocumin, came to Columba one day after the threshing of the corn, but could not look upon his face, it was so brightened by a heavenly glow, and he immediately fled in great fear. Columba called him back, and gently asked him why he had run away so quickly. He replied, "I was frightened." And a while later, being more confident, he asked Columba, "Has any great vision been shown to you in this hour?' And Columba answered, "Such a terrible catastrophe has happened in a remote part of the world!" "What catastrophe?" Asked the youth, "And in what country?" Columba replied, "A sulphurous flame has come upon a city of the Roman Empire. Nearly 3,000 men besides a number of mothers and children, have perished. And before the present year is ended, Gallic sailors, coming from the provinces of the Gauls, will tell these same things to you."

These words were proved to be true, for the same Lugbe, going with Columba to the Land's Head (Cantyre), quested the captain and the sailors of a ship that arrived several months later, and was told by them all those things concerning the city with its citizens just as Columba had prophesied.

Notes:

"Gallic sailors" - There was frequent intercourse between Gaul, Britain and Ireland.

"Lands Head" - Cantyre - Fifty miles from Iona by sea.

It is clear from this account that the monks of Iona in the time of St. Columba were in active sympathy and in touch with the brethren in Italy and Gaul.

THE REMOVAL OF A BOAT.

One time, when traveling beyond the "Backbone of Britain" (Drum Alban, the Grampions), and finding a certain little village, Columba stayed there by the entrance of a stream into a lake. On the same night, waking his sleeping companions, he said, "Go quickly and bring at once our boat which you have put in a house the other side of the stream, and bring it to a nearer hut." And they immediately obeyed and did as they were asked.

And when they were again at rest, Columba after a while quietly nudged Diormit, saying, "Go outside the house, and see what is going on in that village where you first put the boat." And Diormit went out and saw the whole village consumed by flames. Returning to Columba, he told him what was happening. Then Columba told the other brothers about a certain enemy (a druid), who had burned the village.

Notes:

"The Backbone of Britain" - The Dorsal Ridge of Drum Alban, the mountain chain between Perthshire and Argyle, the watershed of Scotland, and the division between the Picts on the East and the Scots on the west.

AEDH THE BLACK.

At another time, Findchan, a soldier of Christ, brought with him from Ireland to Britain, wearing the clerical habit, Aedh, surnamed "The Black," a scion of a royal family (a Cruthinian, Irish Pict, by nation), that he might stay with him in his monastery for some years. Aedh the Black, had been a very bloodthirsty man and a murderer, for he had even killed Diormit, son of Cerbal, who was ordained by God's will, to be ruler of all Ireland.

This same Aedh, after some time had passed summoned a bishop, and was ordained irregularly a minister while with Findchan. The bishop did not dare lay a hand upon his head unless first Findchan himself did, but Findchan loved Aedh with mere human affection.

When this ordination was made known to Columba, he was deeply grieved. Then he prophesied concerning Findchan and Aedh this fearful word, saying, "That right hand Findchan has laid upon the head of the son of perdition shall soon rot, and after great pain it shall go before him into the earth for burial;

31

and he himself shall live for many years after the burial of his hand. But Aedh will return as a dog to his vomit and again be a bloody murderer. And at last his throat shall be pierced by a lance, and falling from wood into water, he will drown."

This prophesy was in each case fulfilled. The right hand of the presbyter, Findchan, having rotted through a blow, went before him into the earth, and was buried in the island called Ommon; but he himself lived for many years after.

But Aedh the Black, priest in name only, returned to his former wickedness and he was treacherously pierced by a lance and fell from the prow of a raft into the water of a lake and perished.

Notes:

"Findchan the presbyter" - His life is given by Colgan, "*Acta Sanctorium*," A.D. 1645

"Artchain" - was a hill in the Ethican land, the island of Tiree. Tiree was much frequented by the Christians of Ireland. Saints Brendan, Cainnech, Comgall, and Colmanela all visited it.

"Aedh, the Black" - Sprung from a royal family, Cruthinian by nation. Aedh Dubh, son of Suibhne of the Dal Araidhe, who inhabited parts of Antrim and Down and were also known as the Cruithene. He was chief of that tribe A.D. 565, King of Uladh A.D. 581- A.D. 588.

"Diormit, son of Cerbal" - Diarmid MacCearrbhal's death is recorded in the Irish Annals.

PART ONE - PROPHETIC GIFT

Notes:

Notes:

PART TWO - MIRACLES

THE WINE MADE FROM WATER.

Columba, as a youth, was staying in Ireland with St. Findbar (or Finnian), the bishop, learning the wisdom of the Scriptures. One day, there was no wine for the communion service, and when Columba heard the ministers complaining among themselves about it, he took the cruet and went to the spring to draw water. In faith, he blessed the water, calling on the name of our Lord Jesus Christ, who, in Cana of Galilee, turned the water into wine. And Christ, working in this miracle, granted to Columba also the changing of water into wine.

He returned from the spring and, entering the church, set down the cruet containing the wine near the altar, and said to the ministers, "Here is wine for you, which the Lord Jesus has sent for the celebration of Communion."

When this became known, the Bishop and the ministers gave great thanks to God. This was one of the first miracles the Lord worked through his young disciple, Columba.

Notes:
"St. Findbar, the bishop" - Probably St. Finnian of Moville, who, with another abbot, Finnian of Colard, in Meath was one of the teachers of

Columba. The ancient *Irish Life of Columba* refers to this very miracle as having occurred when he was studying under Finden (Finnian of Moville).

BITTER FRUIT TURNED INTO SWEET.

There was a tree laden with apples near the monastery of Oakwood Plain and the inhabitants made some complaints about the excessive bitterness of the fruit. Columba approached it one day in the autumn, and seeing that the apples from the tree made the people sick, he raised his hand in a blessing, saying, "In the name of the omnipotent God, let all the bitterness depart from you and be your apples changed into sweet ones." Wonderful to say, all the apples on the tree lost their bitterness and developed into sweet ones.

Note:

St. Mochoemoc performed a similar miracle as narrated by Colgan in *"Acta Sanctorum" P. 593b*.

A BOOK THAT COULD NOT BE DAMAGED BY WATER.

At another time, a *Book of Hymns for the Week*, written by the hand of Columba, was inside a leather satchel and fell from the shoulders of a certain boy who was crossing a bridge and sank in a river of the district of the Lagenians (Leinstermen).

This little book remained in the water from Christmas until Easter and was afterwards found on the bank of the river by some women. They carried the satchel, which was not only wet but rotten, to Iogenan, a minister, whose property it formerly was. And Iogenan, opening the satchel, found his book as clean and dry as if it had remained all that time in a desk and had never fallen in the waters.

I, (Adamnan) have learned from other witnesses that similar things happened in various places with regard to books written by Columba. These books did not decay in unfavorable circumstances.

Concerning this particular book of Iogenan, I (Adamnan), have received the account without any ambiguity from certain truthful men of good repute who inspected the book, which, after all those days under water, was quite white and bright.

WATER BROUGHT FORTH FROM THE ROCK.

When Columba was on one of his journeys, an infant was presented to him by his parents for blessing, and because in that place there was no water to be found, Columba, turning aside to the nearest rock, prayed a little while on bended knees, and rising up, he blessed the brow of the rock, from which water bubbled up and flowed forth abundantly. In it he at once blessed and baptized the infant. Concerning the child he prophesied, saying, "This little boy will live long, to a very old age. In his youthful years he will be slave enough to carnal desires but afterwards he will be devoted to Christian warfare to the end of his life. He will depart to the Lord in good old age."

All these things happened according to the prophecy. This was Lugucencalad, whose parents were in Artdaib Muirchol, where even at the present day there is a health-giving well called after Columba.

A POISONOUS SPRING.

When Columba was staying for some days in the province of the Picts, he heard a report that was spread abroad among the heathen people concerning a spring which foolish men whose senses the devil had blinded, worshiped. For those who drank of that spring or washed their hands or feet in it were smitten by demonic power and became either leprous or blind or else weak or lame; because of all this, the heathen worshiped the spring, because of the demonic power of it.

One day Columba went boldly up to the spring, and seeing this, the druids, whom he himself had often sent away defeated, greatly rejoiced, because they thought that he would suffer the same things from contact with the noxious water. Raising his holy hands and calling of the name of Christ, he washed his hands and feet, then with his companions, he drank of the same water. From that day the demons departed from the spring, and it never again injured anyone. But many people were healed from various diseases.

COLUMBA'S DANGER ON THE SEA.

Another time, Columba was in peril at sea, for the whole hull of the ship was violently tossed about on huge masses of waves. There was a great storm and violent wind everywhere, driving them. Then the sailors said to Columba as he tried with them to empty the bilge-hole, "What you are doing will not help much; you should pray for us, as we are perishing." Columba ceased to empty out the water and began to pour forth fervent prayer to the Lord. And standing in the bow of the ship with his hands outstretched to heaven, he prayed to the Almighty. The whole storm of wind and fury of the sea were stilled and ceased immediately, and instantly an absolute calm ensued. They who were in the ship were amazed and gave thanks with great wonder, and glorified the Lord in Columba.

ANOTHER PERIL AT SEA.

Another time, at the height of a furious and dangerous storm, when his companions cried out for Columba to pray for them, he told them, "On this day it is not for me to pray for you for this danger, but for the Abbot Cainnech."

At that same hour, the Holy Spirit revealed it to Cainnech in his monastery (which in Irish is called Ached-bou), and he heard with the ear of his heart the voice of Columba. Just after the ninth hour he had begun to break bread in the refactory, and he hurriedly left the table with one shoe clinging to his foot and the other (on account of his haste), left behind. He went hurriedly to the church, saying as he went, "It is no time for us to dine now when the ship of Columba is in danger at sea. For at this moment he is calling on God for me to pray for him and his companions in danger."

Having entered the oratory, he prayed for a while on his knees, and the Lord heard his prayer. The storm immediately ceased, and the sea became calm. Then Columba, seeing in the Spirit Cainnech's hastening to the church, (though Cainnech was far away), spoke saying, "Now I know, God has heard Cainnech's prayer, for I see him in a vision run to the church with one shoe, and now God will greatly profit us."

In this miracle, the prayer of both Godly men contributed.

Note:
"St. Cainnech.." - Born A.D. 517 died A.D. 600. Called in Scotland, Kenneth, a famous Saint, native of Keenaght, in County Londonderry, where his principal church at Drumachose was.

THE STAFF LEFT BY CAINNECH AT THE HARBOR.

Cainnech was about to sail from the harbor of Iona to Ireland, and he forgot to take his staff with him. The staff was found on the seashore after his departure and given into the hand of Columba, who on his return home carried it into the oratory, and there for a long time he remained in prayer. Cainnech approaching the Oidechan Island (Islay), was saddened inwardly because of his forgetfulness.

But after some time, disembarking from the ship and bending his knees in prayer on the shore, he suddenly found before him, the staff which he had forgotten on the Island of Iona. And he was amazed, and gave thanks to God at its being transported by divine power.

Note:

Two ancient Celtic staffs, or croziers, have survived to our day; the crozier of St. Filian, long preserved at Strathfillan in Perthshire, and that of St. Molouc, or Moloc, of Lismore, Ireland, now in the possession of the Duke of Argyle.

FAVORABLE WINDS.

Baithene and Columban went to Columba at the same time, asking him to pray for them and obtain from the Lord a favorable wind on the next day, as they were to set out in opposite directions. Columba replied, "Tomorrow morning, Baithene, when you sail out of the haven of Iona, you will have a favorable wind until you reach the port of the Plain of Lunge, (in Tiree)." The Lord granted the favorable winds, according to Columba's word.

At the third hour of the same day, Columba called Columbanus the minister, saying, "Now Baithene has arrived safely at the desired port, prepare yourself to sail now; the Lord will soon change the winds to the north." And at the same hour the south wind, obeying the word of Columba, changed into a northerly direction, and so on the same day each of the men sailed forth with full sails and favorable breezes in different directions. This miracle was done, by the power of Columba's prayers, for as it is written, "All things are possible to him that believes."

After the departure of Columban, Columba spoke this prophetic word concerning him, "The Godly man, Columban, whom we blessed on his departure, will nowhere in this world see my face again." The word proved true, for in that same year Columba passed away to the Lord.

Note:

"Columban, minister" - This was Colman Ela, or Columanellus, born in Glenelly, County Tyrone, A.D. 555, who died in his monastery of Lynallym, (near Tullamore, Kings County) , A.D. 611.

FISHES PREPARED BY GOD FOR COLUMBA.

When some hardy fisherman had taken five fishes in a net in the river Sale, Columba said to them, "Cast your net again in the river, and immediately you will find a large fish which the Lord has prepared for me." And they obeyed the word and drew up a salmon of great size.

At another time, when Columba was staying near Lough Ket, his companions desired to go fishing, but he prevented them, saying, "Today and tomorrow no fish will be found, but I will send you on the third day, and you will find two large river salmon caught in the net." And so after two days, casting the net, they drew to land two very large fish from the river Bo (Boyle).

Notes:

"The River Sale" - Either the Blackwater in Meath, anciently Sael, or Sele, or the Shiel in Scotland flowing out of Loch Shiel.

"Lough Key.." - County Roscommon.

"The River Bo.." - The Boyle which joins the Shannon sea.

NESAN, THE CROOKED.

This man Nesan, though he was very poor, on one occasion joyfully received Columba as his guest. When he had entertained him as hospitably as his means could afford, Columba asked him how many cows he had. "Five," he replied. Then Columba said, "Bring them to me that I may bless them." When the cows were brought, he lifted up his hands and said, "From this day forth, your five cows will increase to 105." And because Nesan was a man of humble birth with a wife and children, Columba conferred upon him also another blessing, saying, "Your seed will be blessed in children and grandchildren." Both prophetic words were completely fulfilled.

Note:

In a manuscript of the 15th century, now in the British Museum, (Royal Collection, No.8d ix), the following is added here. " On the other hand, to a rich but very mean man, Uigene by name, who had despised Columba and had not received him as a guest, he uttered this prophetic sentence, "But the riches of that miser, who has condemned Christ in the strangers seeking his hospitality, from this day shall gradually decrease and shall be reduced to nothing; and he himself shall beg; and his son shall go about from house to house with a half-empty purse, and he shall be struck by some rival with an axe in the pit of a threshing floor and die." Both of these things were completely fulfilled, according to the prophecy of Columba.

THE DEATH OF WICKED MEN WHO MOCKED COLUMBAN.

Columba greatly loved Columban and the virtue of his life and had made him rich, for Columba had rendered to him many acts of kindness.

There was at that time a certain man, an evildoer, a persecutor of good men, Ioan by name, a son of Conall, son of Domhnall, from the royal race of Gabran. This man persecuted Columban and acting with hostility, devastated his homestead-not once but twice, and carried off all he could find.

After a third plundering of that home, while returning to his ship with his comrades and laden with spoil, he met Columba. And when Columba reproached him for his evil deeds and told him to set down his plunder, he stubbornly refused. Boarding the ship with the booty, he mocked him and sneered at him. Columba followed him as far as the sea and walking into the crystal waters up to his knees, with both hands raised to heaven, he earnestly prayed to Christ, who confirms his saints who glorify Him.

Now the harbor in which he prayed was called in Irish Ait-Chambas Art-Muirchol (Camus-an- Gaa Ardnamurchan). When his prayer ended, he returned to dry land and sat down with his companions on high ground, and in that same hour he uttered terrible words saying, "This churl who has despised Christ in His servants will never return to the harbor from which he has just set forth; but neither will he arrive with his wicked accomplices at the other shores, for he will be stopped by sudden death. Today a furious storm, which you will soon see arising out of a cloud in the north, will overwhelm him with his comrades; not one of them will survive to tell the tale."

After waiting a little while on the calmest of days, a cloud arose from the sea as Columba had said, with a great squall of wind. Finding the robber with his spoil between the islands of Mull and Colonsay, the storm suddenly plunged Ioan into the midst of the raging sea, not one of them escaped.

Note:
"Ioan, son of Conall of the royal race of Gabran.." - Gabran was king of the Scotic Dalriada in 558 A.D.

IONA BLESSED BY COLUMBA.

In the same summer season in which he passed away to the Lord, Columba went in a wagon to visit the brethren who were engaged in manual labor in the western plain of the island. After speaking comforting words to them, he prophesied saying, "From this day, my children I know that you will never be able to see my face again in the fields of this plain." And seeing them greatly saddened and trying to console them as much as he could, he raised his hands and blessed the whole island saying, "From this present moment, the poison of vipers will not in any way have any power to harm either men or cattle within the borders of this island, so long as the inhabitants who dwell here will observe the commands of Christ."

Notes:
"The western plain" - Now called Machar.

"The poison of vipers" - No snakes or vipers have ever been seen in Iona, though they are quite common on the opposite coast.

DIORMIT'S CURE.

Diormit, Columba's faithful attendant, was sick unto death, and Columba came and visited him when he was dying. He stood at the sick man's bed and, praying for him, called on the name of Christ. He said, "Be kind to me, I pray, Lord and take not the soul of my faithful attendant from its dwelling while I yet survive." After this he was silent for a while, and then he said, "My servant will not die now, but will also live many years after my own death." And this prayer was heard, for Diormit immediately recovered his full health and also lived for many years after Columba's passing away to the Lord.

THE HEALING OF FINTAN.

When Columba was making a journey beyond the Dorsal Ridge of Britain (Drum Alban, the Grampions), a youth named Fintan was seized with sudden illness and was brought near to death. His sad friends begged Columba to pray for him, and he took compassion on them and spread forth his hands to heaven with earnest prayer and, blessing Fintan, said, "This youth for whom you intercede will enjoy a long life and after the death of all of us present, will survive and live to a good old age."

This prophecy was completely fulfilled, for the same youth later became the founder of the monastery called Kailli-au-inde. He ended this present life in a good old age.

Note:
"Fintan ...founder of Kailli-au-inde" - there are 21 Fintans in the Irish

calendar, and this does not seem to be one of them. Dr. Reeves (Translater of 1857 edition of Columba) thinks that because he joined the monastery in Iona, his history belongs to the North British church.

A BOY RAISED FROM THE DEAD.

When Columba was staying in the province of the Picts, a certain countryman who, with all his household, heared the word of Life through an interpreter, believed and was baptized. After a few days' one of the sons was attacked by severe illness and was close to death.

When the Magi (druids) saw him dying they began to rail at the parents with great abuse and to exalt their own gods as stronger, trying to prove that the God of the Christians was weak.

When all these things were reported to Columba, he was stirred up with zeal for God and proceeded to the house of the countryman, where the parents were holding the sad funeral rites of their child, now dead. Columba, seeing them greatly saddened, encouraged them, urging them to trust God. And he then asked them, "In what room is the body of the dead boy?" The bereaved father led Columba into the house alone, where, on bended knees and with his face bathed in tears, he prayed to Christ. Then rising, he turned his eyes to the dead boy, saying, "In the name of the Lord Jesus Christ, arise and stand upon your feet." At this glorious word, the soul returned to the body. The dead boy revived and opened his eyes, and Columba, holding his hand, raised him up, and steadying him on his feet, led him out of the house and restored him to his parents. Then the shouting of the people arose on high; weeping was turned into rejoicing and the God of the Christians was glorified.

Note:
"Through an interpreter" -This mission seems to have been taken by Columba before he had command of the Pictish language.

BROICHAN THE DRUID AND THE SLAVE GIRL.

Columba requested of Broichan, the Druid, that he set free a certain Irish bondmaid, but with obstinacy, he kept her. Columba addressed him, saying, "Know, Broichan, that if you refuse to deliver to me this captive stranger before I return from this province, you will quickly die."

Saying this in the presence of King Brude, and leaving the royal dwelling, he came to the river Ness and taking a white pebble, he said to his companions, "Note well this white stone by which the Lord will affect many cures among the heathen people." And he added, "Broichan is severely smitten; for an angel sent from heaven has struck him and shattered into many fragments, the glass that was in his hand and has left him gasping and sobbing, nearly dead."

"Let us wait a while in this place, for there are two messengers sent by the king on their way to us. They will ask us to quickly come to help Broichan, who is now ready to set the little maid free." Even while Columba was speaking, two horsemen sent by the king arrived and relayed everything that had happened to Broichan, according to the prophecy . The messengers said,

"The king has sent us to you that you may come to the assistance of Broichan, who is near death, but is ready to free the slave girl".

Columba then sent two of his companions to the king with the white stone, blessed by God, saying, "If first Broichan will promise to free the girl, then let this stone be dipped in water and he shall at once recover health; but if he still refuses, he will immediately die."

When the two companions that Columba sent came to the royal hall, they told the king what Columba had said, the king and Broichan greatly feared. And in the same hour the girl was set free and delivered to the messengers; the stone was dipped in water and contrary to nature, the stone floated on the water. And Broichan drinking from the stone, recovered perfect health.

This remarkable stone, afterwards was preserved among the kings treasures.

Notes:
"Broichan, the Druid" - The name is British

"Royal dwelling" - King Brude's fortified seat was at the north east end of Loch Ness, near modern Inverness, probably on the ridge called Torvean.

COLUMBA'S OPPOSITION TO BROICHAN, THE DRUID.

After these events, Broichan, the Druid, speaking one day to Columba said, "Tell me, Columba, what day are you proposing to sail forth?" "On the third day from now," he replied, "God willing we will begin our voyage." "You will not be able to do so," said Broichan, for I can make the wind contrary and bring dark clouds upon you." Then Columba said, "The omnipotent God reigns over all things, and in His Name all our movements are directed."

On the third day, Columba came to the long lake of the river Ness with a great crowd following him. But the druids began to rejoice when they saw darkness coming over the sky and a tempest, a contrary wind. It should not be wondered at the art of demons (for it was a legions of devils that once met Bishop Germanus in mid-ocean when he was sailing from the Gallican Gulf to Britain. And demons stirred some dangerous storms and spread darkness over the sky and obscured the daylight. All of the storms were stilled by the prayer of Germanus and, quicker than he prayed, it ceased and the darkness was swept away).

Seeing the furious elements stirred up against him, Columba called on Christ and entering the boat with the fearful sailors, confidently ordered the sail to be rigged against the wind. When this was done the whole crowd looked on while the boat was borne along through the contrary winds with amazing velocity.

After a short while, the winds veered around to the advantage of the voyagers, to the astonishment of all. Throughout the rest of the day the boat was driven along by favorable breezes until it reached its desired haven. And so God was glorified among the Christians and the heathen and the druids.

Notes:

"The Bishop Germanus, sailing from the Gallican Gulf." - Germanus, Bishop of Auxerre, visited Britain in A.D. 429 and A.D. 448. The incident of the storm mentioned here is given in *Life of Germanus*, by Constantius, a priest of Lyons, contemporary of Columba.

" The Gallican Gulf" - The British Channl.

THE OPENING OF THE GATE OF A ROYAL FORTRESS.

At another time, when Columba was weary from his first journey to King Brude, it happened that the king, elated by pride in his fortress, did not open the gates at Columba's arrival*. And when the man of God realized this, he came with his companions to the wickets of the portals and traced on them the sign of the Lord's cross and then he knocked and laid his hands on the gates. The locks immediately shot back, the doors opened at their own accord, and Columba entered with his companions.

When this became known to the king, he and his council were very frightened and went to meet Columba with all reverence and addressed him politely.

From that day the ruler honored Columba all the days of his life, which was proper.

Notes:
"Pride in his fortress" - this was probably the fortified ridge of Torvean, near Inverness.

* Not opening the gates for a visitor was considered an insult.

A DEFORMED BOAT PILOT, HATED BY HIS WIFE.

When Columba was a guest on the Rechrean island a peasant came to him and complained that his wife disliked him and would not allow him to approach her. On hearing this, Columba called the wife and began to reprove her, saying, "Why, woman, do you try to drive your own flesh away from you, when the Lord says, 'And they two shall be one flesh?'" She answered, saying, "Anything that you command, however hard, I am ready to do, except one thing; do not ask me to cohabit with Lungne. I do not refuse to do all the housework or, if you bid me, even to cross the sea and remain in some monastery of women."

Columba then said, "That which you speak cannot rightly be done, for you are bound by the law to your husband as long as he lives. For those whom God has lawfully joined, it is a sin to separate." And having said this, he added, "This day let us three pray and fast to the Lord." She then said, "I know it is not impossible for you to obtain by prayer from God those things that seem impossible to men."

The wife agreed to fast with them. The following night, Columba prayed for them all night, and the next day he said, in the husband's presence, "Woman are you prepared today as you said yesterday, to go away to a monastery of women?" "Now I know," she said, "That your prayer to God for me is heard, for him whom I hated yesterday, I love today, for my heart this night past has been changed." And from that day until her death she was indissolubly cemented in love to her husband.

A PROPHECY CONCERNING PEASANT GUIRE.

A certain peasant, a brave man of that time among the people of Korkureti, asked Columba what kind of death he would die. Columba replied, "Not in battle nor on the seas will you die, but the companion of your journeys, of whom you have no suspicion, will be the cause of your death." "Maybe some of my friends may desire to kill me; or my wife, for love of some younger man, may do me to death by foul play," said the man. "That is not how it will happen," said Columba. "I am unwilling to tell you anything more concerning your 'companion,' because the frequent thought of it will sadden you too much. The day will come when you will prove the truth of this word."

After a few years, Guire was sitting one day beneath a boat, smoothing down the point of his spear shaft with his knife, and hearing others fighting among themselves nearby, he quickly got up to part them. As he arose, the knife fell to the ground, and in that sudden emergency, he stumbled, and his knee was severely gashed. Some months later he died from the effects of the wound. And this kind of companion, (his knife), was the cause of his death. He recognized the knife as the 'companion' that Columba had prophesied about.

THE CRANE FROM IRELAND.

When Columba was living on the Isle of Iona, he called one of the brethren to him. "On the third day from now," he said, "You must keep a look-out in the western part of the isle on the seashore, for from the northern region of Ireland, a certain guest, a crane, driven by the winds, will arrive very weary and exhausted after the ninth hour of the day; and it's strength almost gone, it will fall and lie on the seashore. Take care to lift it gently and carry it to a neighboring house, and there they will nurse it and attend to it for three days and nights."

"At the end of the three days, refreshed, it will return with fully regained strength to the sweet region of Ireland, whence it came. And I earnestly commend it to you, for it came from the place of my own fatherland," (Ireland).

The brother obeyed, and on the third day after the ninth hour, he awaited the coming of the unexpected guest; and when it came he raised if from the shore where it fell and carried it to a house nearby, and they fed it and nursed it.

On his return to the monastery in the evening, Columba, not by way of inquiry, but of statement, said, "God bless you, my son, because you have well attended our stranger guest; and it will not stay in exile, but in three days return to it's own country." And, just as Columba prophesied, having been cared for three days, it raised itself on high by flight from the ground and considering for a little while its course in the air, it returned across the ocean to Ireland in a straight line of flight.

Note:

"A certain guest, a crane" - Adamnan was surely right to include this incident in his narrative. *The Lives of the Irish Saints* abound with references to their sympathy and affection for birds. There are stories about cranes in the lives of Saints Finian and Aibhe, and other narratives in the voyages of St. Brenden are full of marvels concerning birds. Stories of favorite animals and the love of animals occur in the lives of the saints in every country.

THE BATTLE IN THE FORTRESS OF CETHIRN.

After the convention of the kings at the Ridge of Ceate (Aedh, son of Ainmire, and Aiden, son of Galran), Columba was returning to the ocean plains. He and the Abbot Comgell sat down not far from the fortress. Water for washing their hands was brought from a fountain nearby. When Columba had received it, he prophesied to Abbot Comgell, "The day will come, Comgell, when that little spring from which this water was poured will not be fit for any human use."

"How will the water from the spring be corrupted?"asked Comgell. Then Columba said, "Because it will be filled with human gore; for my kindred and your relations according to the flesh, which is the Hy-Neill and the people of the Cruithni, will wage war in this neighboring fortress of Cethirn. From there it will come about that in that spring some poor fellow of my family will be slain, and the basin of the spring will be filled with his blood."

After many years this prophecy was fulfilled. And in the battle, Domhnall, son of Eadh, was victorious, and a certain man of his race was slain in the spring, according to the word.

Also many years later another soldier of Christ, Fintan, an Anchorite, was near the monastery of Oakwood Plain relating some things about the same battle. He declared to me, Adamnan, that he saw a dead body in the spring. On that day, returning from the battle, to the monastery of St.Comgell, he found two aged monks to whom he told about the battle and the corrupted spring. They replied at once, "A true prophet is Columba, who, as he sat near the fortress of Cethirn, foretold all you those things of which you are speaking, in our presence and in the presence of comgall."

Notes:

"The fortress of Cethirn.." - named after Kethern, son of Fintan of Ulster. It is now known as the "Giant's Sconce" and is near Colarine.

"The convention of the kings at the Ridge of Ceate." - The convention was held in A. D. 575 at Drum Ceate, a long mound now known as the Mullagh, or "Daisy Hill." It is near Newtownlimavaddy, in County Londonderry. One of the main objects of the convention was the abolition of the bards. It was summoned by Aedh, son of Ainmire, King of Ireland. Aiden, the son of Galran, who was present, was Lord of the Scotch Dalraida in A.D. .574 and the founder of the supremacy of that race in Scotland. There were numerous petty kings and heads of tribes. Columba attended the convention along with his retinue and accompanied King Aiden. The assembly was held not far from Columba's monastery at Derry, and no doubt this retinue would consist of persons taken from his Irish monasteries.

"Abbot Comgell.." - Founder and first Abbot of Bangor, born A.D. 517, died A.D. 602

"The Hy-Neill and the people of Cruithni" - The Ui-Neill, Hy-Neill or O'Neills, descendants of Niall, of Nine Hostages, King of Ireland A.D. 358- A.D. 405. Columba was the great grandson of Conall Gulban. Domhnall, son of Aedh who also descended from Conall Gulban and who led the clans in the battle, was therefore among Columba's "family friends," as he said. The Cruithni were the Irish Picts who held the southern part of Antrim and most of Down. Abbot Congall was ninth in descent from Fiacha Araidhe, founder of the race, and Congal Claen, who commanded the Dalradians in this battle was tenth in descent from the same individual.

"In the battle of Domhnal" - fought in A.D. 629

"Another Soldier of Christ, Fintan by name" - There are many saints recorded with that name. Colgan (*Acta Sanctorum*) believed that the Fintan mentioned here was Fintan Lobhar, who founded many monasteries in Munster and Leinster and died in the reign of King Finachta, A.D. 674-A.D. 693. Oakwood Plain is Durrow.

Notes:

PART THREE - ANGELS

COLUMBA'S BIRTH.

One night just before the birth of Columba, an angel of the Lord appeared to his mother while she was asleep, and standing by her, brought her a mantle of great beauty, in which the colors of all the flowers were depicted; after a brief interval, he asked for it back, and took it from her hands, and raising and spreading it out, sent it forth into the air. She was saddened and asked, "Why do you so quickly take away this lovely mantle?" He immediately replied, "The reason is that this mantle belongs to one of honorable station." And at these words the woman saw the mantle gradually receding from her in its flight, and increasing in size to as to exceed the width of the plain and to overtop the mountains and forests; then she heard a voice say, "Be not sorrowful, you shall bring forth a son, like one of the prophets of God, and he will be numbered among them, and is predestined by God to be the leader of innumerable souls to the heavenly country." And while she heard this voice, the woman awoke.

Note:
"Increasing in size (the mantle)" - the old *Irish Life of Columba,* describes the mantle as reaching from the Inishymoe Islands in Clew Bay, on the coast of Mayo, to the Northeast Coast of Scotland.

A LUMINOUS RAY SEEN ON COLUMBA'S FACE.

On another night, Cruithnechan, the foster-father of Columba, returning after church to his home, found his entire house irradiated by bright light; for he saw a globe of fire stationary over the face of the little sleeping boy. And seeing it, he immediately trembled with fear, and falling with his face on the ground in great wonder, he understood that the grace of the Holy Spirit was poured out from heaven upon his foster-child.

Notes:

"Cruithnechan" - The name is a diminutive of Cruithnech (Pict). It does not occur in the Irish Calendars, but there is a parish in County Derry now call Kilcronaghan, i.e.Kill Cruithnechan.

"The Church" - This was Killmicnenain, anciently Doire-Ethne, and now Kilmacrenanm in County Donegal. The churches connected with the history of St. Columba's early life are all in this neighborhood, namely, Gartan, where he was born; Tulach Dubhaglaisse, now Temple Douglas, where he was baptized by the Cruithnechan here mentioned; Killmicnenain and Rath-enaigh, where he was instructed by Bishop Brugach.

THE ANGELS BRENDAN SAW.

After a long period of time, when Columba was excommunicated by a certain synod for some unjust causes (as afterwards became clear), he came to the same assembly that was convened against him. And when Brendan, the founder of that monastery, which is called in Irish, Birra (Birr), saw him approaching, he quickly rose and with his face bent down, reverently kissed him. And when some seniors of that assembly chided him and said, "Why did you rise up and kiss one who is excommunicated?" he replied, "If you had seen those things which the Lord has shown to me this day regarding Columba, you would never have excommunicated one whom God highly exalts." They said, "We would like to know how God does exalt him whom we have excommunicated, and with good cause."

"I have seen," said Brendan, "An exceedingly bright pillar going before Columba and holy angels also accompanying him in his walk on the plain. I dare not, therefore slight this man, whom I see ordained by God to be a leader of nations unto Life." When he had said these words, not only did they desist, not daring further to excommunicate Columba, but they honored him.

These things were done in Teilte (Teltown, Meath).

Notes:

"Excommunicated by a certain synod" -There is no means, says Dr. Reeves, of ascertaining with certainty the date of this synod or the acts of Columba which it condemned. It was possibly in A.D. 561 after the battle of Cul dremhne, and Columba's action in bringing about that battle may have been the reason for the excommunication.

Brendan" - Founder of Birr. He must be distinguished from Brendan, founder of Clonfert and voyager. They were both contemporary friends of Columba. Brendan of Birr died in A.D. 573. Birr is now Parsonstown.

"These things were done in Teilte"- Teilte, now Teltown, between Kells and Navan in County Meath was famous in old times for a great fair. It was also a seat of royalty, so that the monarch of Ireland was sometimes called "King of Teilte." The ruins of a church and the remains of large Rath and other ancient works distinguish the site.

THE ANGEL WHO WAS SENT TO COLUMBA THAT HE MIGHT ORDAIN AIDAN AS KING.

When Columba was staying in Hinba island (Eilean-ma Maoimh), one night in a spiritual ecstasy he saw an angel of the Lord, who held in his hand a book of glass of the Ordination of Kings, and when Columba received it from the angel's hand, at his command he began to read it. And when he refused to ordain Aidan as king according to the direction given in the book (because he loved Iogenan, Aiden's brother, more), the angel suddenly stretching forth his hand, struck Columba (the mark of which stayed all his life), and then spoke these words, "Know for certain that I am sent to you by God with this book and that according to the words you have read in it, you may ordain Aidan to the kingship; and if you will not obey this command, I will strike you again."

The angel of the Lord appeared for three successive nights, having in his hand the glass book and pressing the commands of the Lord concerning the ordination of that king. Columba obeyed the word of the Lord and sailed across to the Isle of Iona, and there, as he had been commanded, he ordained Aedhan (Aidan) as king (who arrived there at the same time). And during the words of ordination he *prophesied future events regarding his sons and grandsons and great grandsons, and laying his hand upon Aidan's head he ordained him as king and blessed him.

Notes:
"Prophesied" * Cuimine the fair, seventh Abott of Iona, wrote in his book, *Devirtatlilus Sancti Columbae* concerning the virtues of Columba. He said that Columba began to prophecy to Aedhan, and his posterity and his

kingdom saying, "Believe, O Aedhan, without doubt, that none of your adversaries will be able to resist you, unless you first do wrong to me and to those who come after me. Therefore commend to your sons and grandsons and posterity, lest through evil councils they lose from out of their hands the scepter of this realm. For, if at any time they do anything against me or against my kindred, who are in Ireland (the mark of which I have endured from the angel), their cause shall be turned upon them by the hand of God, to their great disgrace; mens hearts shall be withdrawn from them, and their enemies shall be greatly strengthened over them." Now this prophecy was fulfilled in the battle of Roth, when Domhnall Brecc, grandson of Aedhan, devastated without cause the province of Domnhall, grandson of Ainmire. And from that day to this they are in decadence through pressure from without.

Devirtatilus Sancti Columbae - This book was incorporated into ADAMNAN'S Life of St. Columba.

"A book of glass.." Some commentators think that this ceremonial book is called " *Liber Vitreus*" because the cover of it was covered with glass or crystal.

"Iogenan, brother of Aedhan.." - he died A.D 595.

"**The battle of Roth**" - Magh Rath, either Moira in Co. Down or the neighborhood of Newry. That battle was fought in A.D. 637 as is recorded in the *Annuls*, and in an ancient historical romance called, "*The Battle of Magh Rath,*" published in the original Irish, with translation and notes for the Irish Archaeological Society in A.D. 1842 by Professor O 'Donovan. The battle continued with varying success for six days, and on the seventh, the Irish king, Domnhall, son of Aedh, son of Ainmire, cousin of St. Columba, was victorious, Domnhall Brec, King of the Irish Scots, hardly escaped to Britain with the remains of his army. He was defeated in another battle by the Picts in Glen Morison.

"They are in decadence" - The scepter passed to the house of Loarn, after the house of Ganhran had suffered many reverses, of which the rival families of the race took advantage, the Picts, Strathclyde Britains, and the Saxons profiting by the decline of the Dalriadic power.

THE ANGELS WHO ASSISTED COLUMBA IN A BATTLE AGAINST DEMONS.

When Columba was living in Iona, he went into the woodlands to be alone for prayer, and there, as he afterward told a few of the brethren, when he began to pray, suddenly he saw a very black host of demons fighting against him with strong darts. And as it was revealed by the Spirit, they wished to invade his monastery with their fiery darts in order to kill many of the brethren. But he, one man against many devils, taking up the armor spoken of by the apostle Paul, fought in brave conflict. And so for the greater part of the day, the war was waged on both sides. The many demons could not vanquish the one; nor was he alone strong enough to drive them from his island until the angels of God came to his aid, and for fear of them, the terror stricken demons quitted the place.

On the same day, Columba returned to the monastery after the flight of the demons from his island. He spoke this word, saying, "Those deadly foes who have been put to flight from the boundaries of this territory have gone to the Ethican land (Tiree), and they shall there, like savage invaders, attack the monasteries of the brethren and bring about diseases, by the virulence of which many shall be attacked and die." And this came to pass according to the prophetic foreknowledge of Columba.

And after a two-day interval Columba said by revelation of the Spirit, "Baithene has, by God's help, managed to defend the congregation of the church over which he presides in the Plain of Lunge (Tiree). He has by fastings and prayers kept away the invasion of the demons, for no one except the one already dead will die this time."

And this was fulfilled, according to Columba's prophecy. Apart from the one already dead, there were no more that died in Baithene's monastery.

Note:
"The armor of the apostle Paul." The armor of God as described in the Scriptures (Ephesians, chapter six).

A MANIFESTATION OF ANGELS CONCERNING THE DEATH OF BRENDAN.

While Columba was living in Iona, he called Diormit, his attendant, early in the morning and commanded him, saying, "Let the elements for Communion be made ready quickly, for today is the birthday festival of the blessed Brendan." "Why do you command that such solemn celebration of Communion be prepared for today? For no messenger has brought any news of the death of Brendan from Ireland." Then Columba said, "Go; obey my order, for last night I saw heaven suddenly opened and choirs of angels descend to meet the soul of Brendan; and by their incomparable brightness, the whole area was illuminated."

Notes:
"Birthday festival" - The birthday of the future state; the death-day on earth.

"Blessed Brendan.." - Reference has already been made to him. He died A.D. 573 in his 80th year. November 29th is his festival day.

A VISITATION OF ANGELS CONCERNING A DROWNING.

When Columba was living in Iona, he was roused by a sudden impulse, and getting the brethren together by the sound of the bell, he said, "Now, let us pray for some monks of the Abbot Comgell, who are drowning in the Lough of the Calf (Belfast Lough), for at this moment they are warring in the air against hostile powers who are trying to snatch away the soul of a stranger who is drowning along with them." Then, after tearful and earnest prayer, he said joyfully, "Give thanks to Christ, for now the holy angels have met those souls, and have delivered that stranger guest and triumphantly rescued him from the warring demons."

Note:

"The monks of the Abbot Comgell" - St. Comgell's great monastery of Bangor, according to the *Ards of Ulster*, was founded in A.D. 558. The churchyard alone remains to mark the site, but its ancient "Antiphonary" of the eighth century is preserved at Milan. An interesting account of it is given by Dr. Reeves, in the first volume of the *"Ulster Journal of Archaeology"* Belfast 1853.

THE ANGEL WHO HELPED A BROTHER WHO FELL.

While Columba was sitting writing in his hut, his countenance suddenly changed and he cried out, "Help! Help!" then two brethren standing at the door (Colgu, son of Cellash, and Luge Mocublai), asked him the cause of his cry. Columba answered, "I have directed the angel of the Lord, who was just now standing among you, to go quickly to help one of the brethren who has fallen from the roof of a building in the Plain of the Oak Wood (in Ireland)." And Columba then added this, "Very marvelous is the swiftness of angelic flight, like lightning, for that angel who just now flew away from us came to his help when he was beginning to fall, and in the twinkling of an eye, held him up before he could touch the ground. Nor does he who fell have any fracture or bruise.

THE ANGELS WHO CAME FOR A CONFERENCE WITH COLUMBA.

Columba assembled the brethren together and charged them, saying, "Today I wish to go alone to the western plain of our island; therefore, none of you should follow me." And they complied, and he went alone. But a certain brother, going by another way, secretly posted himself on the top of a certain hillock that overlooked the same plain, desiring to find out why Columba wanted to go alone.

And the spy saw Columba standing on a mound on that plain praying with his hands spread out to heaven. Suddenly, the brother saw many holy angels, clad in white garments, bright citizens of the heavenly country, flying to Columba with wonderful swiftness. They began to stand around him as he prayed. And after some conversation with the blessed man, that celestial band sped quickly back to heaven.

And Columba, having returned to the monastery after the angelic conference, and the brethren being assembled, he inquired with sternness, which of them was guilty of disobedience. And protesting, they said they did not know.

But the one who was conscious of his transgression and no longer able to hide his fault, asked forgiveness. Columba, leading him aside, charged him that he must not reveal anything, even the least particle of that angelic visitation, to anyone while he was alive.

But after the departure of Columba from this world, the brother related the account to the others with solemn witness. To this day the place of that angelic conference attests to the event that took place by it's proper name, which in Latin is "Colliculus Angelorum" (Hill of Angels), but in Irish, "Cnoc Angel."

It should be understood how great and excellent and numerous were those sweet angel visits to Columba, safeguarding him on the winter nights when he was in lonely places.

Notes:
"A certain hillock- that overlooks the plain"...No doubt the eminence now known as Cnoc Orain, between the monastery and the plain, commanding a view of the plain and Columba's standpoint.

"A certain mound on that plain." - Colliculus Angelorum, Cnoc Angel, the Hill of the Angels, referred to before. The mound now known as Sithean Mor, a round knoll of sand, covered with green sward, on the left of the little road which leads to the western shore of Iona.

A VISITATION OF THE HOLY SPIRIT THAT REMAINED OVER COLUMBA FOR THREE DAYS AND NIGHTS.

When Columba was dwelling in the isle of Hinba (Eilean - na - Naoimh), the anointing of revelation wonderfully rested upon him for three days and nights. He remained neither eating nor drinking within the house, which was filled with celestial brightness, and he would allow no one to approach. And from this same house, rays of intense brilliancy were seen at night bursting from the chinks of the doors and the keyholes. And certain hymns which had not been heard before were heard being sung by him. Afterwards he declared in the presence of a few people, that he had seen openly manifested many secrets hidden since the beginning of the world.

And some obscure and difficult passages of the scriptures became plain and clear to the eyes of his heart. He complained that his foster-son, Baithene, was not present, for if he had been there during those three days, he might have written down many revelations from his lips; mysteries concerning past ages or those which were to come. Baithene, however, could not be present, as he was detained by a contrary wind in the isle of Egea (Eigg).

Note:
"The Isle of Egea." Eigg, 40 miles north of Iona. St. Donnan, an Irishman and disciple of St. Columba, founded a monastery there, and in A.D. 617 perished with his community of 51 persons in an attack by pirates. The church of the island is named after him, Kill-Donan.

THE BRIGHT LIGHT VIRGNO SAW IN THE CHURCH.

Virgno, burning with the love of God, entered the church alone to pray while the others were asleep. He went to a side chamber and began to pray devoutly. After an interval of about an hour, Columba entered the church also, and along with him, a golden light descended from heaven and filled all that part of the church. The brightness of the same celestial light, bursting through the inner door of that chamber, which was just a little ajar, filled the interior of the little side chamber where Virgno was doing his best to hide himself. And as no one can gaze directly upon the noonday sun, so also Virgno could not bear the brightness. He was greatly frightened at the sight this splendor and no strength remained in him. Columba, after prayer, left the church.

And the next day he called Virgno (who was very much alarmed) and addressed him in these consoling words, saying, "Well pleasing have you been in God's sight this night past, my child, casting down your eyes to the ground, terrified as you were by the fear of His brightness, for had you not done so, your eyes would have been blinded by the sight of the pure light. But this you must carefully observe, never to disclose to anyone in my lifetime this manifestation of light." And so it was that after the passing away of Columba, this remarkable event became known to many through the same Virgno.

Comman, an honorable minister priest, son of Virgno's sister, gave to me Adamnan, an attested account of the above recorded vision. And he also had heard the same account of it from the lips of his uncle, the Abbot Virgno.

Notes:

"Virgno".. - Also Fergno. This was Fergno Brit, fourth Abbot of Iona, A.D. 605- A.D. 623. He was descended from Enna Boghaine, who gave his name to Boghainigh, now Banagh, in western Donegal.

"Comman.." - This was the brother of St. Cuimine Fionn, seventh Abbot of Iona.

VISION OF BRIGHTNESS FROM ABOVE.

One of the brethren, Colgius by name, son of Aedh Draignichi, came by chance to the door of the church while others were sleeping, and standing there, prayed for a while. And then he saw the whole church filled with celestial light, which vanished quickly. He did not know however, that Columba was in the church praying at the same time. And after this sudden vision of light, he returned home in great fear. The following day Columba, calling him, sharply rebuked him, saying, "You should take care from this time, my son, that you do not attempt to see the heavenly light which has not been granted to you, because it will escape you; and tell no one in my days what you have seen."

ANOTHER VISION OF DIVINE LIGHT.

Columba one day gave strict orders to a certain pupil of his, Berchan by name, surnamed Mesloen, saying, "Take care, my son, that you come not near my little dwelling tonight, as you are accustomed to do." And Mesloen, hearing this, went, despite the prohibition of Columba. And put his eyes straight to the keyhole, expecting that some celestial vision would be manifested within. For at that same hour, that little dwelling was filled with the splendor of heavenly brightness; and, not able to bear the sight of it, the young trespasser instantly fled.

The next day, Columba led him aside and rebuked him in these words, saying, "Last night, my son, you did sin before God, for you foolishly thought that your crafty spying could be hidden from the Holy Spirit. Did I not see you at that hour coming to the door of my dwelling? And had I not prayed for you in that same moment, you would have fallen dead before the door or blinded. But the Lord has spared you this time for my sake. But know this, that you shall live riotously in your native Irish land, and thereafter your face shall blush with shame all the days of your life. But this I have obtained from the Lord in my prayers, that because you are our foster child, you shall repent in tears before your death and obtain mercy from God."

All these things happened to him afterwards, according to the prophetic words of Columba.

A VISION GIVEN TO COLUMBA WHEN HE WAS ABOUT TO LEAVE HIS BODY.

One day while Columba was living on the isle of Iona, his face blossomed into wonderful and joyful cheerfulness and, raising his eyes to heaven, he was filled with great delight and rejoiced greatly. Then after a brief interval, that sweet rejoicing was turned to sadness.

Two men who were standing at the door of his hut (Luge Mocublai and the other a Saxon, Englishman called Pilu,) inquired as to the cause of his gladness and subsequent sorrow. Columba said, "Go in peace, and do not now ask of me that the cause of the joy or the sorrow be made known unto you." On hearing this, they knelt in tears and begged him to let them know something of what had been revealed at that time. And seeing them greatly saddened he said, "Because I love you, I am loathe you should be sad, but you must first promise not to disclose to any man during my life the secret that you ask about." And they immediately promised according to his injunction.

Then Columba spoke to them, saying "This present day, 30 years of my sojourn in Britain are completed. Meanwhile for many days past I have devoutly asked my Lord Jesus that He would release me from my time here and call me at once to my heavenly country. And this was the cause of my rejoicing. I saw holy angels sent from the throne on high to meet me and lead forth my soul from the flesh. But they suddenly stopped and are standing on a rock on the other side of the Sound of our island, desiring to approach and call me away from the body. But they are not permitted to come nearer, and they must soon return to heaven. For that which the Lord granted to me, (namely, that on this day I should pass away from the world to Him), was quickly altered, yielding to the prayers of many churches for me. And to these churches, it has been granted by the Lord (though against my will), that four years from this day are added to my life in the flesh. This was the cause of my sorrow today.

And when, please God, these four years in this life are ended, my passing away shall be sudden, without any bodily illness, and I shall depart rejoicing to the Lord in the company of the holy angels who will then meet me."

According to these words that Columba uttered (not without much sorrow and with many tears), he lived for four years more.

Note:
These events occurred in A.D. 593, thirty years after Columba's settlement on Iona.

THE PASSING AWAY OF COLUMBA.

Toward the end of the four years, one day in the month of May, the old man, weary with age, was carried on a wagon to visit the brethren while at their work. He spoke to them, saying, "During the Easter festival, in April, I desired to pass away to Christ the Lord, as He has invited me. But lest your festival of joy should be turned into sadness, I preferred that the day of my departure from the world be put off a little longer." The monks of his household were very sad when they heard these words, and he began to cheer them as much as he could with words of comfort.

Turning his face eastward, he blessed the island and the islanders. And from that day, the poison of vipers has been powerless to do any harm to man or beast. After those words of blessing, Columba was carried back to his monastery.

Then after a few days, while Communion was being celebrated on the Lord's Day, suddenly, with eyes raised heavenwards, Columba's countenance was seen to be suffused with a ruddy glow, just as it is written "When the heart is glad, the countenance blossoms" (Prov:15:13). For in that hour he saw a bright angel of the Lord hovering above, within the walls of the oratory. When those who were present asked what the cause of his gladness was, Columba, gazing upward, gave this reply; "Wonderful and incomparable is the presence of the angelic nature. For behold! An angel of the Lord was sent to fetch a certain deposit, dear to God, and after looking down upon us and blessing us, he has returned again."

None of the bystanders realized what the nature of that 'deposit' was, which the angel was sent to claim. But Columba gave the name of a 'holy deposit' to his own soul, which had been entrusted to him by God.

And so at the end of the week, that is on the Sabbath day (Saturday), he and his dutiful attendant, Diormit, went to bless the granary that was nearby. And he spoke these words, saying, "Greatly do I congratulate the monks of my household that this year, for when I depart from you, you will have enough for the year, without need." And hearing these words, Diormit began to be sorrowful and said, "Often you make us sad at this time of year because you make mention so often of your leaving us."

Columba replied, "I have a certain secret chat to hold with you, and if you will firmly promise to tell no one before my death, I shall be able to tell you something more clearly about my leaving." And when Diormit had made the promise,

Columba said, "In the *Sacred Volumes*, this day is called the Sabbath, which is interpreted-rest. And this day is truly a Sabbath day for me because it is for me the last day of this present life, and then I will rest from my labors. And this night at midnight, when begins the Day of the Lord, according to the scriptures, I shall go the way of my fathers (Josh.23:14, 1Kgs 2:1-2). For already my Lord Jesus deigns to invite me and to Him I will depart in the middle of this night." Hearing these words, Diormit began to weep bitterly, and Columba tried to console him.

After this Columba, returning to the monastery, sat down halfway at the place where afterwards a cross in a millstone (standing to this day), is to be seen at the roadside. And while Columba, rested there, the white horse, a faithful servant ran up to him, (the one that used to carry the milk pails to and fro between the byre and the monastery). The white horse, amazing to tell, laid his head upon Columba's breast, inspired as I believe by God, by whose grace every animal has sense to understand things as its Creator has ordained.

Knowing that his master was soon to leave him, he began to whinny and shed tears into Columba's lap, as though he had been a man. And Diormitt began to drive away the weeping mourner. But Columba said, "Let him alone, let him alone, for he loves me, let him pour out the tears of sadness into my bosom. For you as a man, possessing a rational soul, could in no way know anything about my departure (except what I have just now told you), but to this beast, devoid of reason, the Creator Himself has clearly in some way, revealed that his master is about to go away from him." and he blessed his servant the horse, as it sadly turned away.

And ascending the hill that overlooks the monastery, he stood for a little while on its top, and raising both hands, he blessed his monastery saying, "Upon this place, small though it be, not only the kings of the Scotic people (i.e. the Irish of Ireland and Britain) with their peoples, but also the rulers of barbarous and foreign races shall confer great honor here; even also those of other churches shall give great reverence to it."

After these words, and returning to the monastery, he sat in his hut transcribing the Psalter. He came to that verse of the 33rd Psalm (v.11), where it is written, "But they that seek the Lord shall not want any good thing." "Here," he said, "I must stop at the foot of this page and what follows let Baithene write."

The last verse he had written is very applicable to the dying saint, to whom the good things of eternity shall never be lacking; and the verse that follows is indeed very suitable to the Father who succeeded him and was the teacher of his spiritual sons, namely; "Come, ye children, hearken unto Me; I will teach you the fear of the Lord," For Baithene succeeded him not only as teacher, but also as a writer.

After transcribing the verse at the end of the page, Columba entered the church for the evening service, and as soon as this was over, he returned to his cell and sat up throughout the evening on his bed, where he made the bare rock for a pallet and stone for a pillow, which to this day stand by his grave as his monumental pillar.

And so, sitting up, he gave his last commands to the brethren, saying, "These are my last words I commend to you, O my sons: that you have mutual and unfeigned charity among yourselves, with peace; and if, according to the example of the holy Fathers, you will observe this, God the comforter of the good, will help you; and not only will the necessaries of this present life be sufficiently supplied by Him, but the rewards of the good things of eternity, prepared for those who keep His divine commandments, shall also be given abundantly."

This, in brief narrative, are the last words of our Columba as he was passing away to the heavenly country. As happily the last hour gradually approached, he was silent. Then, when the bell began to toll at midnight, he rose in haste and went to the church, running faster than the others, he entered it alone. Then on bended knees, he fell down in prayer at the altar.

At the same moment, Diormit, who followed more slowly, saw from a distance the whole church filled with angelic light. And as he drew near to the door, the light he had seen suddenly withdrew. This light a few others, who stood some distance away, also saw.

Diormit, entering the church, cried with a mournful voice, "Where are you Father?" And as the lights of the brethren had not yet been brought, and he, groping his way in the dark, found Columba lying before the altar, and raising him up and sitting down by him, he laid his head on Columba's bosom.

Meanwhile, the community of monks, returning with the lights, began to weep at the sight of their dying Father. And as we have learned from some who were present, Columba, his soul not yet departed, with open eyes upturned, looked around on either side, with wonderful cheerfulness and joy of countenance on seeing the holy angels coming to meet him. Diormit then lifted up the right hand of the saint that he might bless the choir of monks. But Columba himself, at the same time moved his hand as much as he was able, so that what was impossible for him to do with his voice, at his soul's departure, he might still do by the movement of his hand, namely, give his last blessing to the brethren. After this he immediately breathed forth his spirit.

And having left the tabernacle of his body, his face remained so ruddy and wonderfully gladdened by the vision of the angels that it seemed to be of one not dead, but living. Meanwhile, the whole church resounded with sorrowful crying.

In the same hour, Columba's passing away was revealed to a certain saint in Ireland. For in the monastery which in the Irish is called Cloni-finchoil (The meadow of the white hazel; perhaps Rosnarea, on the Boyne), there was a certain man, a veteran soldier of Christ, who was named Lugud, son of Tailchan. This man early in the morning, sadly told to another soldier of Christ, (Fergno by name), a vision of his, saying, "In the middle of this past night, Columba, pillar of many churches, passed away to the Lord. In the hour of his departure I saw in the spirit the island of Iona, all resplendent with the brightness of angels--the whole space of the sky, up to the heaven of heavens, was illumined by the splendor. Angels sent from heaven, came down in troops to bear his soul to heaven. High-sounding hymns, also, and exceeding sweet songs of the angelic hosts did I hear at the same moment that his soul departed amid the angelic choirs as they soared on high."

Virgno (Fergno) who rowed over in those days from Ireland and remained for the rest of the days of his life in the isle of Himba often narrated to the monks of Columba this angelic vision, which he had heard himself from the lips of Lugud.

And Virgno after many years passed blamelessly, and in obedience among the brethren, and completed 12 more years in a place of Anchorites in Muirbulcmar (Himba?). This above mentioned vision we have not only found recorded in books, but we have also learned from several well-informed, aged men, to whom Virgno himself had told it.

At the same hour also there was another vision revealed. A soldier of Christ, one of those who witnessed it, related with solemn witness to Adamnan, when he was a youth. He was a very old man whose name was Ferreolus, but in Irish Ernene (diminutive of Iarn, iron) of the clan Mocuffirroide, who himself was a monk and is buried in the Ridge of Tomma (Drumhome, in Donegal).

He said, "On the night on which Columba passed away from earth to heaven, I and those with me, while fishing in the valley of river Fend (Finn in Donegal), saw the whole expanse of sky suddenly illuminated; and struck by the suddenness of this miracle, we turned our eyes to the east, and there appeared to us an immense pillar of fire, rising upward at that midnight hour. It seemed to lighten the whole world, just like the summer sun. And after the pillar penetrated the heavens darkness followed, and not only did we who were present see the brightness of this luminous and wonderful pillar of light, but many other fishermen who were scattered, fishing in various pools of the river.

The miracles of these visions, which appeared the same hour Columba passed away, bear witness to the eternal honors conferred upon him by the Lord.

Meanwhile, after the departure of Columba, the evening service being ended, his body was carried with singing from the church to the house, and for three days and nights his funeral rites were performed with due observance, with sweet praises to God. His body was wrapped in a fair shroud and placed in a tomb; buried with due reverence to rise again in eternal brightness.

Now, near the close of this book, shall be told what has been handed down to us by well informed persons concerning those above mentioned three days' obsequies which were carried out in the usual ecclesiastical form. Indeed, one of the brethren, speaking in all simplicity in the presence of venerable men, said to Columba, "After your death, all the people of these provinces will sail across and fill this little isle of Iona." Hearing this, Columba said, "O my child, the event will prove otherwise, for a promiscuous crowd of common people will by no means be able to come to my funeral, only the monks of my own house will perform my burial rites, and honor my funeral offices." God caused this prophesy to be fulfilled, for immediately after his passing away (during those three days), there arose a great tempest of wind without rain, which prevented anyone from crossing over the Sound from the other shore.

And after the burial was over, the tempest was at once stayed, and the wind ceased, and the whole sea became calm.

Let us consider how great an honor Columba enjoyed in the sight of God, when at times God granted his prayer that storms be stilled and seas be made calm. So also the winds were changed at the close of his funeral. Such then was the end of Columba's life.

To use the words of scripture, he shares in eternal triumphs; he is linked with the apostles and prophets and is joined to the thousands of white-robed saints who have washed their robes in the blood of the Lambkin; he follows the Lamb wherever He leads; he is a virgin without spot, free from all stain, through the favor of the Lord Jesus Christ, to Whom, with the Father, is honor and power and praise and glory and everlasting rule, in the unity of the Holy Spirit, for ever and ever.

Notes:

"During the Easter festival" -Easter day fell on April 14th in A.D. 597, in the year of Columba's death.

"At the place where afterwards a cross, fixed in a millstone, is to be seen" The cross known as MacLean's Cross in Iona is the only one now remaining on the island whose position corresponds to the description in the text. Mr H.D. Graham, (In *Antiquities of Iona*, A.D. 1850) says, "To the south of the cathedral there is a cross of a very ancient date. It is one of stone about 11 feet in height, including the pedestal. It is of the hardest whinrock, and although it has the appearance of great age it is very little impaired. This cross is of a different form, and apparently of a different era from any other in the Highlands."

"Ascending the hill that overlooks the monastery" -The original monastery was about 300 yards to the north of the medieval ruins and the hill called Cnoc-na-bristeadh-clach, which is just outside the remains of the Vallum.

"Upon this place...kings..shall confer honor"- Iona was in fact the chosen burial place of many kings. It is stated in the *Scotichronicon* that the monastery of the monks of Iona was the burial place and royal seat of almost all the Scotic and Pictish kings to the time of King Malcolm, the husband of St. Margaret (she died A.D. 1093). Sir Donald Monro, who was High Dean of the Isles and visited most of them in A.D. 1549 mentions "three tombs of staine formit like little chapels" as existing in the cemetery, Relig Oran on Iona, inscribed respectively in Latin as Tombs of the Kings of Scotia, Hybernia and Norwegia; 48 Scottish, 4 Irish and 8 Norwegian kings, says Sir Donald, "According to our *Scots and Erische cronikels*" are these buried.

"A stone for a pillow" a stone marked with a cross and exactly of a form suitable for a pillow is still shown at Iona as that of St.Columba. It was found by Mr. Alexander McGregor within twenty yards of the large boulder of granite under which St. Columba is said to have been buried. A part of the stone was broken off by a farmer's cart passing over it. A cross is indeed incised upon it. Mr Drummond was inclined to regard this stone as the one Adamnan referred to. It is now in the Abbey.

It would appear that at least a century elapsed before Columba's remains were disinterred. They were enshrined, however, before the year A.D. 824, as we learn from Walafridus Strabo's ninth-Century verses on the martyrdom of St. Blaithmac of Iona, in the Danish invasion. (See Messinham's *Florilegium Insula Sanctorum, 1624, p.402*) St. Blaithmac was brutally murdered in A.D. 825 because he refused to disclose the hiding place of Columba's remains.

"As we have learned from some who were present" - St.Columba died in A.D. 597, and St. Adamnan was born in A.D. 624, so the information of eye witnesses was quite easily available to Adamnan.

THE DOMINIONS OF COLUMCILLE

IONA

ORKNEY

Dun I
Relig Odhrain
Dun Bhuirg
Hill of the Angels
Spouting Cave

OUTER HEBRIDES

Craig Phadrig

PICTLAND

CANNA
RHUM
EIGG
Ardnamurchan
COLL
TIREE
MULL
LISMORE
IONA
COLONSAY
ORONSAY
JURA
ISLAY

Mechtanschene
Dunkeld

Dumbarton

FIRTH OF FORTH

STRATHCLYDE

NORTHUMBRIA

Lindis
Bamburgh

Jarrow
Wearmouth

Rathlin Island
Dun Cethirn
Drum Ceatt
Derry
Raphoe
Gartan
DONEGAL
ULSTER

Whithorn

Moville
Cladnevny
Armagh
Down

Lough Neagh

CONNAUGHT

Kells
Tara
Clonard
Clonmacnoise
Durrow
Kildare
LEINSTER

84

About David and Kathie Walters

David and Kathie are originally from England. They spent 11 years under the ministry of the famous expositor Dr. Martin Lloyd-Jones, of Westminster Chapel in London.

After being baptized in the Holy Spirit in 1969 they became involved in a revival. Out of this they began to evangelize the schools, first of all locally and then all over the U.K. They saw many hundreds of children and youth saved, and filled with the Spirit.

They came to live in the U.S. in 1977. David travels extensively to churches and conferences, bringing a vision to include the children in the move of God and bringing them into a powerful anointing. He sees God use the young people in an awesome way in his miracle services.

Kathie ministers at womens conferences and churches. Kathie has a burden to release women in their potential, in the anointing and calling on their lives. She ministers on the grace of God and deliverance from the spirit of religion.

Other Products Available from Good News Ministries

Children's Illustrated Bible Study Books
The Armor of God, Fact or Fantasy,
Fruit of the Spirit, and *Being a Christian*

Books for Parents, Teachers, Children and Youth Pastors
Kids in Combat, Equipping the Younger Saints,
Children Aflame, The Anointing and You
and Parenting-By the Spirit.

Other Books by Kathie Walters
Living in the Supernatural, The Visitation, The Spirit of
False Judgment, Parenting-By the Spirit, and Celtic
Flames.

Exciting Teaching Tapes and Videos Available

GOOD NEWS MINISTRIES
220 Sleepy Creek Road
Macon, Georgia 31210

Phone (912) 757-8071
Fax   (912) 757-0136
e-mail: goodnews@hom.net
Web: www.goodnews.netministries.org

Call or write
for more information
on Kathie Walters'
new book
Celtic Flames

Good News Fellowship Ministries
220 Sleepy Creek Road,
Macon, GA 31210
Phone (912) 757 8071
Fax. (912) 757 0136
e-mail ADDRESS: goodnews@hom.net
WEB SITE: goodnews.netministries.org

Notes:

PART THREE - ANGELS

Notes:

COLUMBA-THE CELTIC DOVE

Notes:

PART THREE - ANGELS

Notes:

Notes:

PART THREE - ANGELS

Notes:

Notes:

PART THREE - ANGELS

Notes:

Notes: